GARDEN SQUAD!

GROWING FLOWERS

WILLIAM DECKER

PowerKiDS press™

New York

Published in 2016 by The Rosen Publishing Group, Inc.
29 East 21st Street, New York, NY 10010

First Edition

Editor: Sarah Machajewski
Book Design: Michael J. Flynn

Photo Credits: Cover Tatiana Grozetskaya/Shutterstock.com; back cover, pp. 3–4, 6, 8–9, 12, 14–18, 21, 23–24 (soil) Andrey_Kuzmin/Shutterstock.com; p. 5 matka_Wariatka/Shutterstock.com; p. 7 (seeds) PhilipYb/Shutterstock.com; p. 7 (plants) Thana Nattribhop/Shutterstock.com; p. 7 (flowers) JIPEN/Shutterstock.com; p. 9 motorolka/Shutterstock.com; p. 10 Mr Twister/Shutterstock.com; p. 11 (flower photo) Anna Breitenberger/Shutterstock.com; p. 11 (flower illustration) BlueRingMedia/Shutterstock.com; p. 12 Supachita Ae/Shutterstock.com; p. 13 Shaiith/Shutterstock.com; p. 15 (marigolds) sakchaistockphoto/ Shutterstock.com; p. 15 (petunias) GeNik/Shutterstock.com; p. 15 (begonias) Wutthichai/Shutterstock.com; p. 15 (lavender) napat uthaichai/Shutterstock.com; p. 15 (black-eyed Susans) maxstockphoto/Shutterstock.com; p. 15 (peonies) Sea Wave/ Shutterstock.com; p. 17 gorillaimages/Shutterstock.com; p. 19 NinaMalyna/ Shutterstock.com; pp. 20, 21 anat chant/Shutterstock.com; p. 22 Diana Taliun/ Shutterstock.com.

Library of Congress Cataloging-in-Publication Data

Decker, William (William Anthony), 1983- author.
  Growing flowers / William Decker.
      pages cm. — (Garden squad!)
  Includes bibliographical references and index.
  ISBN 978-1-4994-0949-9 (pbk.)
  ISBN 978-1-4994-0966-6 (6 pack)
  ISBN 978-1-4994-1012-9 (library binding)
  1. Flower gardening—Juvenile literature. 2. Flowers—Juvenile literature. I. Title. II. Series: Garden squad!
  SB406.5.D44 2015
  635.9—dc23
                                            2015007073

Manufactured in the United States of America

CPSIA Compliance Information: Batch #WS15PK: For Further Information contact Rosen Publishing, New York, New York at 1-800-237-9932

CONTENTS

BEAUTIFUL FLOWERS............ 4

SEED TO FLOWER 6

THE OUTSIDE OF A FLOWER....... 8

THE INSIDE OF A FLOWER........10

PICKING THE PLACE 12

ANNUALS AND PERENNIALS 14

START PLANTING 16

CARING FOR PLANTS 18

POLLINATION................... 20

A GARDEN OF POSSIBILITIES..... 22

GLOSSARY 23

INDEX........................ 24

WEBSITES 24

BEAUTIFUL FLOWERS

What comes to mind when you think of a garden? Many people think of flowers. Though there are many kinds of plants to grow, flowers may be one of the most **rewarding**. Flowers aren't just enjoyable to look at and smell. They also play an important part in the natural world.

Flowers are a great choice for people who are new to gardening. However, it takes some knowledge of plants and a little bit of **patience** in order to grow them properly. Armed with these two things, you'll grow a garden full of beautiful flowers in no time at all.

GARDEN GUIDE

There are over 300,000 species, or kinds, of flowering plants in the world. They make up about 80 percent of all plants!

Flower gardening is easy once you get the hang of it.

5

SEED TO FLOWER

Flowers begin as seeds. It's hard to imagine something so small could produce a beautiful plant, but it's true. Seeds are different shapes, sizes, and colors, depending on the kind of flower they come from.

Seeds have a hard covering that **protects** the seed's inside, which contains everything a plant needs to grow. With enough water and sunlight, a seed sprouts into a tiny plant called a seedling. The seedling grows into an adult plant, and the adult plant produces a flower. The flower makes seeds, which grow plants, which grow more flowers. This life cycle is what gives your garden its beautiful plants.

GARDEN GUIDE

A life cycle is all the stages a living thing goes through from birth until it dies.

THREE STAGES
OF CHRYSANTHEMUMS

Growing flowers is a great way to learn about every stage in a plant's life cycle.

THE OUTSIDE OF A FLOWER

Just like their seeds, flowers themselves look very different. However, they all have the same parts. Let's look at a basic plant to learn about its parts and why they're important.

Every plant has roots. Roots keep a plant firmly in the soil. They also take in water and **minerals**, which plants need to live. The roots are connected to the stem. The stem keeps the plant upright. Water travels through the stem to the leaves. Leaves take in sunlight and carbon dioxide, which is a gas in the air. Plants need these things to live. Many plants also have colorful and **fragrant** flowers. Some plants may make fruit, but gardeners usually don't plant them in flower gardens.

GARDEN GUIDE

Plants take in sunlight and air through their leaves. They use them to make their own food. This is called photosynthesis.

FLOWER BUDS

FLOWERS

STEM

LEAVES

ROOTS

Look closely at the leaves of your adult plants. You may see flower buds growing among them. Over time, they'll open into beautiful, colorful blooms.

THE INSIDE OF A FLOWER

When you look at a flower, you may first notice its beautiful color or great smell. Color and smell come from the petals. Petals **attract** birds, bats, and bugs. They also surround and protect the inside of the flower.

The inside of a flower contains the parts needed to make new plants. They're called the stamen and pistil. The stamens make pollen. They're long and thin. The pistil has several parts. The top, called the stigma, collects pollen that comes from other flowers. The bottom is where the flower makes seeds. Some flowers have both stamens and a pistil, but others may only have one or the other.

STIGMA

POLLEN

STAMEN

PISTIL

PARTS OF A FLOWER

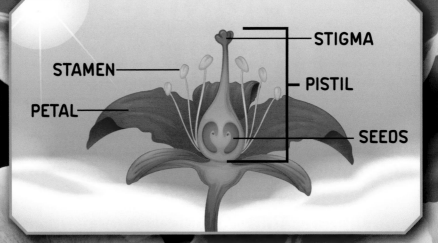

STIGMA

STAMEN

PISTIL

PETAL

SEEDS

PETAL

STIGMA

STAMEN

PISTIL

Understanding the parts of a flower makes
growing them more fun.

11

PICKING THE PLACE

To get started, pick where you'd like to plant your flowers. Planting flowers in certain areas around your yard or house can improve the way it looks. You can choose a **plot** in your yard and plant many kinds together. Some gardeners plant flowers along the sides of their house. You can also grow flowers in single pots or

in hanging baskets. Flower boxes are great for planting flowers under windows.

Flowers come in all shapes, sizes, and colors. Planting a **variety** of them is a good way to keep your garden or yard looking great.

ANNUALS AND PERENNIALS

What kind of flowers do you want to grow? Garden flowers are sorted into two groups—annuals and perennials. Annuals die after one year. This allows you to change how your garden looks, since you can try planting something different each year. Marigolds, petunias, and begonias are some examples of annuals.

Perennials bloom for many years. Perennials are a good choice if you want the same plant to grow in the same spot every season. Also, planting perennials can help you save money since you don't have to buy them every year. Lavender, black-eyed Susans, and peonies are popular perennials.

Planting annuals and perennials gives you a chance to practice caring for both.

MARIGOLDS

LAVENDER

PETUNIAS

BLACK-EYED SUSANS

BEGONIAS

PEONIES

START PLANTING

Now that you know how a flower lives and grows, it's time to get ready to plant. Ask an adult to help you choose a place for your garden. Most flowers need a lot of sunlight, so pick a place in your yard that gets between six and eight hours of sunlight a day.

Once you've chosen your spot, it's time to prepare the soil. Make sure it isn't dried out and that it **drains** well. Many gardeners add special soils to their garden beds to make sure plants have enough **nutrients**. Finally, choose what flowers you'd like to plant, and get digging!

It's not always easy to grow flowers from seeds. You can buy baby plants from the store and replant them in your garden.

GARDEN GUIDE

Some flowers need a little bit of shade, or a lot, to grow well. Check with other gardeners or your local nursery, which is a place that grows and sells plants, to find out what your flowers need.

CARING FOR PLANTS

Part of being a great gardener is tending to your plants. You can't just plant something and then forget about it! Like any living creature, plants need care in order to be their best.

The best way to care for your flowers is to get outside and handle them. Check to see if the soil is wet enough. Dry, cracked soil isn't good for flowers. Cut away any brown or dead leaves or blooms. Keep your flowers safe from critters that will eat them by putting up a fence or netting.

GARDEN GUIDE

Some plants may not flower the first year you plant them. It may take a few seasons for your hard work to pay off.

Trimming dead leaves and blooms from a plant is called pruning.

19

POLLINATION

Once you plant a flower garden, you'll spend some time watering and caring for your plants. However, one of the most important parts of your garden's success is something nature takes care of—pollination.

Pollination happens when pollen from one flower is carried to another, which causes the flower to make seeds. This happens in many ways. Bees and butterflies that visit flowers in search of nectar also pick up pollen. They then carry the pollen to other flowers as they fly around. Other pollinators include the wind and people and animals that brush against flowers.

Invite pollinators to your garden by planting flowers with attractive petals and strong smells.

GARDEN GUIDE

When flowers die, seeds fall to the soil, and new plants grow. Gardeners may also take a flower's seeds and plant them in the spring.

A GARDEN OF POSSIBILITIES

Growing flowers is very rewarding. They look pretty and smell great. Flowers give food to important creatures, such as bees, butterflies, and birds. Your flower garden is an important part of their habitat, or natural home, so remember—you're not the only one who enjoys it.

There are many ways to use your flowers. Cut a few blooms to keep in your house. Pick flowers for a friend, or keep them planted outside for your neighbors to enjoy. At the end of the season, think about what you want to grow next year. The possibilities are endless!